RISE AND SHINE

Empowering Affirmations for Boys and
Young Teenagers of Melanin

Rev. Dr. Yvette A. Armstead

Cover designed by Kendell X. Rouse

ISBN 979-8-89243-041-8 (paperback)
ISBN 979-8-89243-042-5 (digital)

Christian Faith Publishing
832 Park Avenue
Meadville, PA 16335
www.christianfaithpublishing.com

Printed in the United States of America

In the vibrant pages of *Rise and Shine: Empowering Affirmations for Boys and Young Teenagers of Melanin*, a transformative journey awaits. Step into a world where positivity, self-love, and resilience take center stage, offering a guiding light to young minds of color. Through an array of uplifting affirmations, this book celebrates the brilliance and potential within each individual, inspiring them to embrace their unique identities, conquer challenges, and reach for the stars. With every turn of the page, boys and young teenagers of melanin will discover the power of their thoughts, unlocking a world of limitless possibilities. Let the journey begin, as these affirmations become the foundation for a life filled with confidence, strength, and unwavering self-belief.

This incident will forever haunt me. My son was going through a difficult time during his first year of college, and I mistook it for typical challenges of growing up. However, he was crying out for help. We had a terrible argument, and in the midst of it, he said, "No one asked me why my eyes are x——— out, not even you care about me." This was profoundly alarming and devastating as a mother because I believed I knew my child well and we had a strong relationship.

He showed me a painting, and like his other artwork, it was terrific. Little did I know, this painting was a desperate plea for help. That's why we must affirm our young men of color, let them know we love them, value them, and believe in their future and God-given purpose. Now whenever I see my son, I smile, and I make sure to tell him I love him every single time we talk. Things could have taken a different, darker turn, but by the grace of God, we are here. Let us affirm our young boys, teenagers, and men of color, reminding them they are worthy. Every day, let's tell them how much we love them.

In the heartfelt pages of *Rise and Shine: Empowering Affirmations for Young Men of Color*, we embark on a crucial mission to support and uplift the mothers and grandmothers raising these remarkable individuals. In a world where their skin color is unjustly perceived as a threat, it is imperative to provide guidance and strength.

As a single mother who courageously raised three children, two of whom are African American young men, sleepless nights became a familiar companion. The constant worry about their safety when they ventured out with friends weighed heavily on my heart.

The unimaginable trauma that our young men of color endure is terrifying, leaving mothers and grandmothers on their knees, praying for their protection and well-being.

Within these affirmations lies the power to instill belief in our young boys, young adults, and young men, even when the world may deem them unworthy. They are reminded that their worth stems from being created in the image of our Lord and Savior, gifted with a rich heritage. They are descendants of kings and queens, carrying a legacy of greatness within them.

You, young men of color, are inherently worthy. Embrace these affirmations as a guiding light, reminding you of your immense value, strength, and potential. May they empower you to rise above adversity, defy stereotypes, and pave your path toward a future filled with success and fulfillment.

Rev. Dr. Yvette A. Armstead

Micheal Brown
Trayvon Martin
Eric Garner
Freddie Gray
Philando Castile
Walter Scott- Laquan McDonald
Alton Sterling
Stephon Clark
Botham Jean
Ahmaud Arbery
George Floyd

    This book honors the lives of these young men of color and inspires others, particularly young, melanated individuals, to understand their heritage and recognize the importance of their lives. It aims to celebrate their legacies and highlight the ongoing struggle for justice and equality.

Our branches are only as strong as the roots we come from.

The concept of affirmations reminds us that our branches, or the aspects of ourselves that are visible to the world, are only as strong as the roots we come from. In other words, our foundation and beliefs about ourselves greatly influence our growth and success.

Day 1

For God so loved the world that he gave his only begotten Son, that whoever believes in him should not perish but have everlasting life.

— John 3:16

To our dear boys of melanin color, you are loved, cherished, and unique in your abilities. God has a plan for your life, a plan of hope, and a plan for a future because you are worthy and wonderfully made. You are not alone in this journey called life. He will never leave you nor forsake you. Whatever others say about you casts all your anxieties and fears upon him. Talk to your loved ones and express your hurts and desires. Yet, always remember that God above will sustain you. Our Lord has given you a spirit of power, love, and a sound mind. Remember, when this world casts you down and says you are not worthy, you have control and a sound mind. Talk to God because you can trust in him, renew your strength, and he will give you the strength and the courage you need to press on. Be strong and courageous, for the Lord is with you.

Day 2

I am fearfully and wonderfully made, wonderful are
your works, and my soul knows it very well.

Psalm 139:14

My extraordinary diamonds of the earth, you are valuable and precious in the eyes of the Lord. The God we serve and who created you is mindful of everything you do and will always reward you for your faithfulness even when you feel like no one loves you, you feel alone, and the people you trust don't protect you. He is your source of strength and will always uphold you with his right hand of righteousness. You can trust and depend on him to guide your steps and give you the courage and determination to succeed. When this world tells you you are not worthy and you are nothing. Be encouraged and that the Lord is with you even when family, friends, and loved ones have turned against you. Know the Lord is always with you.

Day 3

I can do all things through Christ who strengthens me.

—Philippians 4:13

Know that you come from queens and kings, my young princes. You are worthy, and you have greatness embodied in you. You are endowed with gifts that should be used to serve others and to empower others to walk in greatness.

You are empowered by the strength of Christ, who dwells in you. You can do all things through him who gives you power. When you are told that you are not smart enough, when you are told that you are not qualified, when you are told you cheated on a test that you know you studied for, and you made the grade, when you are told you are not lovable, and you are taught self-hate. Regardless of the challenges you face, remember that you are not alone. God's power and grace are there for you, helping you to overcome any obstacles that may come your way. Have faith and trust in your abilities because they are God-given, and you can achieve greatness. Always remember God is with you; you can achieve anything when you put your mind and heart into it. You can rise above all things, my prince, and fulfill your purpose with confidence and tenacity. Believe in yourself. Know your worth. For you are fearfully and wonderfully made. You are beloved, beloved.

Day 4

No weapon formed against you shall prosper, and every tongue
which rises against you in judgment you shall condemn.

—Isaiah 54:17

My beautiful prince of greatness, no weapon formed against you shall prosper, for the divine shield protects you. You are the beacon of strength. You have the agility to overcome and think with your mind and the essence of your natural power.

You are intelligent with a mind that is creative and inspiring. Learn to embrace your heritage. Learn from your elders and read to know how rich and talented your ancestors were. Know your worth, and stand on the shoulders of those who have come before you. Have pride and confidence in yourself and where you come from. You come from excellence, and you are destined for greatness. You are a young man with limitless potential, capable of achieving anything you set your mind to. Your dreams are your dreams, and they are valid. You can rise above any challenges that you may face. You are loved, supported, and worthy of success, my beloved prince.

Day 5

For you created me inmost being; you knit
me together in my mother's womb.

—Psalm 139:13

As a young man of melanin, you are God's unique and valuable creation. Embrace the melanin of your beautiful skin, your roots that carry the blood of your ancestors, and the strength that is passed from one generation to another with the trauma that is passed, causing a new heartbeat to rectify the past and a flow of passion that has been given to you.

My prince, you are beautifully crafted with your melanin with a purpose and a destiny that you, my prince, have been chosen to complete. My child of melanin dismisses any negative stereotypes or prejudices that try to diminish your worth. Stand tall, my prince, be proud of your heritage, and show your talent and worth to the world. Do not be ashamed. You are intelligent, capable, and deserving of every opportunity that comes your way. You will and can rise against any challenges, breaking down barriers placed before you. You have a light that shines brighter than the sun and illuminates like the moon in the darkness of the night. You are an inspiration to others. You may melanated prince is paving the way for generations to come. You are a beacon of hope, a symbol of the strength of your skin's melanin. Your gifts will be challenged, but you, my beloved prince, will use your skills and talents to make a positive impact and create a lasting change in your family, the community, and the world. My beautiful diamond fearfully and wonderfully makes you of melanin. Continue to embrace who you are, be proud of your heritage, love yourself, and walk this life confidently and gracefully.

Day 6

Let no one despise your youth, but be an example to the believers
in word, in conduct, in love, in spirit, in faith, in purity.

—First Timothy 4:1

You are a pillar of strength, courageous, and capable of being a positive role model in a world that sees you as a threat. You, my child, cannot let the views of others cause you to look down on yourself because you are beautiful, and your skin holds the melanin of strength that causes your skin to become the life of the things you touch. I encourage you, my beloved, to have standards and to set standards to be an example to others in your actions, with your speech, in love, by your faith, and with your purity. Strive to inspire and encourage those around you—showing them your beauty, worth, and creative mind. Your worth and your creative mind. Your value is not defined by your clothes, socioeconomic status, or family, but your character's content determines it. Embrace your unique identity in this world and use your platform to bring about change and make a difference in the world. Do not allow what people say to you affect you; do not let negative stereotypes or prejudices define you and a lack of a moral compass represent you. My melanated young man, rise above the naysayers and prove you can achieve greatness. Pursue your dreams, chase after your passions, and work hard to reach your God-given potential. Celebrate who you are, your heritage, and the rich diversity within your soul. You are a melanin boy/young man who is wonderfully and fearfully made. Walk with pride into your purpose, creating a lasting impact in your community.

Day 7

Trust in the Lord with all your heart and lean not
on your own understanding, in all your ways.

—Proverbs 3:5–6

As a new day awakens, my prince, trust in the Lord with all your heart
and do not lean to your limited understanding. This world will try to
keep you focused on material things, but the Lord our God wants you
to focus on heavenly things. Every day, he allows you to take a breath
and seek his divine guidance in all your ways, knowing that he will
direct your path. You are not defined by expectations and stereotypes
but by your belief and faith in our God. Embrace the approach set
before you, knowing that you will have many challenges and victories
in this life journey—knowing that you are never alone. You are embodied with a mind, body, and soul guided by a higher power that sees
your worth, potential, and purpose. Young men of melanin, fearlessly
pursue your dreams and know that all things are possible with God on
your side. This thing called life comes with many bumps, bruises, and
crying. When you know that God is leading the way, you have a future
filled with a promise. Be strong, my prince, capable and resilient, ready
to face whatever the world throws. You are brilliant, my young men of
melanin. Trust God in all ways so that your steps and path are straight.

Day 8

For I know the plan I have for you, declares the
Lord, plans to prosper you and not to harm you,
plans to give you hope and a future.

—Jeremiah 29:11

My young brilliant light of melanin, despite the challenges you face here, God has a plan for your life filled with hope, prosperity, and a future. Do not let the pain or trauma define you; do not be angry. You are a survivor by the blood that runs through your veins. You are worthy of healing and restoration despite whatever trauma you have endured.

My child of melanin, we often find ourselves in situations where we have experienced trauma that we do not understand, and it causes harm because it is passed from one generation to another. My beautiful child of the sun, if you have experienced addiction-related trauma. If you find that addiction has infiltrated your life, you are not defined by it. My diamond of melanin, you are strong and capable of breaking free from its grips. Speak up and be determined to seek the necessary help, resources, and support, not to let the addiction of parents, friends, or yourself take your power. You can overcome the addiction and regain control of your life. You are not alone in your journey. God is with you every step of the way, providing love, strength, and guidance.

My beautiful child of the earth, life sometimes hands us hands where life stressors cause us not to handle life's journey mentally well. Just know, my child, that mental health issues do not diminish your worth or potential. We come from a history where these issues are not discussed, but I want you to know it is okay to seek help and support for your mental well-being. You come from queens and kings who faced many challenges. Face it head-on and seek out the necessary assistance. Mental health challenges do not limit you, my beautiful melanin child; you are resilient and can overcome them.

My beautiful child, we all have family issues; no one is born into a perfect family. We all have experienced some kind of fear, trauma, and pain and have gone through turmoil. Recognize my beautiful child of melanin in your skin and the power it emits. You don't need anyone to tap into your beautiful mind for the wrong reasons. Your family issues and circumstances do not define your worth and identity. You are not characterized by the dysfunction or brokenness that surrounds you. You can rise above any and all family struggles, and you can create a future that is God-given. Choose to break generational cycles and build a legacy of love, forgiveness, and strength, my strong, brilliant child of melanin.

You, my sun-brilliant child of melanin, are more than your past or present circumstances. You are a strong, talented young man of color, and never forget to have faith, love, and hope because there is a future that God designs for you. Face these challenges with courage, seek help when needed, and move forward with tenacity and determination. You are resilient, my child of melanin. You are worthy and capable of creating a life filled with love, joy, and purpose.

Day 9

Do not conform to the pattern of this world, but be transformed
by the renewing of your mind. Then, you will test and approve
what God's will is, his good, pleasing, and perfect will.

—Romans 12:12

My melanin, beautiful child of color, I want you to embrace who you
are and know that your skin radiates life with a purpose. I want you
to embrace the passage of Romans 12:12 and refuse to conform to
the negative patterns and stereotypes that society wants to impose on
you. My melanin child of melanin from God, I need you to choose
to be transformed by renewing your mind and by embracing your
uniqueness in your identity and purpose.

You are not limited by the expectations or limitations others
place upon you. You are capable of achieving greatness and pursuing
your dreams. Be confident in your abilities and talents, knowing they
are gifts God gives you. You deserve opportunities; all you have to do
is be willing to work diligently to accomplish your goals and dreams.

Learn to embrace your heritage and cultural background, recognizing the strength and resilience it instills in you that runs through
your blood. Be proud of who you are and where you come from, and
honor the struggles and sacrifices that have paved the way for your
success. You, my beautiful child, carry your legacy with pride and
determination.

My golden child of the sun, you are not defined by the color of
your skin or the circumstances you face, my beautiful beloved. You
are a child of immense worth and potential. Reject society's negative narratives about you because of your glistening, beautiful skin.
Choose to define yourself by God's measurement. Define yourself
based on the content of your character, values, and actions. Know

that your skin and your hair are a representation of your heritage and your strength. You are intelligent, compassionate, and capable of positively impacting the world.

Surround yourself with those who engage in the beauty of the light and who are positive influences. Seek out mentors who believe in and see your greatness. You are not alone. You have a village that loves you, supports you, uplifts you, and wants to encourage you. You are resilient in the face of adversity. Knowing that everything you face, my child of melanin, only strengthens your character and shapes your future.

My child of greatness, commit yourself to always pursuing knowledge, embracing education, and always opening your mind to continuous growth, emotionally and spiritually. Be open to learning and expanding your horizons, knowing that you, my child, will be equipped with the necessary tools to make a difference.

I affirm to you, my child of perpetual golden melanin, that you have a purpose and a meaning. You are here for a reason, and I encourage you to fulfill your destiny. Walk confidently, embracing your uniqueness to make a difference and impact the world positively and knowing that you are destined for greatness.

Day 10

Be strong and of good courage; do not fear or be afraid
of them; for the Lord your God. He is the one who goes
with you. He will not leave you nor forsake you.

—Deuteronomy 31:6

Be strong and courageous, young men of melanin, for the Lord your
God goes with you. He will not leave you nor forsake you. Embrace
your heritage, stand firm in your identity, and know that your life
holds immeasurable value. You are fearfully and wonderfully made,
destined for greatness and purpose. Your voice matters, your dreams
matter, and your contributions to this world are significant. You can
overcome any obstacle with God by your side and shine brightly.
Walk boldly, love fiercely, and remember you are loved, seen, and
cherished. Your journey matters, and you have the power to create
positive change. Keep moving forward, young men of color, for you
embody strength, resilience, and hope.

Day 11

But those who wait on the Lord shall renew their strength;
they shall mount up with wings like eagles; they shall
run and not be wary; they shall walk and not faint.

—Isaiah 40:31

Take heart, young men and boys of melanin color, for those who wait upon the Lord will renew their strength. The struggles you face do not define you but rather the resilience and courage with which you rise above them. God's perfect timing will give you the wings to soar above adversity. Your worth, talents, and potential are immeasurable, and no obstacle can hinder the greatness that lies within you. Embrace your unique identity and heritage, for they are sources of strength and inspiration. Trust in the Lord's guidance and lean on His promises, for He will never fail you. With faith as your foundation, you can accomplish extraordinary things and leave a lasting impact on the world. Rise, young men and boys of color, and let your lives be a testament to the power of resilience, perseverance, and unwavering faith. You are more than conquerors, and your journey is destined for greatness.

Day 12

For God has not given us a spirit of fear, but of
power and of love and a sound mind.

—Second Timothy 1:7

Young boys and men of color, embrace the power within you, for God has not given us a spirit of fear but of power, love, and a sound mind. In this world that may try to diminish your worth or limit your potential, remember that you are fearfully and wonderfully made, with unique gifts and talents to offer. Stand tall and confident in your identity, knowing that your heritage and experiences are sources of strength and resilience. Despite the challenges you may face, believe that you possess the power to overcome them. Let love guide your actions and interactions, for it is through love that you can break down barriers and build bridges of understanding. Cultivate a sound mind, seeking knowledge, wisdom, and discernment to navigate this world with clarity and purpose. Trust in the Lord's guidance and lean on His promises; He is your ultimate source of strength and protection. Your presence in this world is significant and impactful, and you have the power to make a positive difference. Rise above limitations, embrace your true potential, and let your light shine brightly, inspiring others with your courage, resilience, and unwavering faith. You are capable, loved, and destined for greatness. Believe it, embrace it, and let it propel you forward.

Day 13

Let your light shine before men, that they may see your
good works and glorify you, Father in heaven.

—Matthew 5:16

Young melanin boys and men of color, let your light shine before others so they may see your good works and glorify your Father in heaven. In a world that may sometimes try to dim your light or underestimate your potential, remember that you are fearfully and wonderfully made, with unique gifts and abilities to offer. Embrace your identity and heritage with pride, knowing that your presence and contributions are valuable and impactful. Let your actions and the goodness within you speak volumes, inspiring others to see the beauty and strength in your melanin skin. Rise above any challenges or stereotypes that may come your way, for you have the power to break barriers and defy expectations. Use your voice to advocate for justice, equality, and positive community change. Be a beacon of hope, love, and compassion, spreading positivity and upliftment wherever you go. Trust in your abilities and the potential that lies within you, for you can achieve greatness. Remember that your worth is not defined by the opinions of others but by the content of your character and the love you share with the world. Let your light shine brightly, illuminating the path for others and glorifying our Heavenly Father. You are a powerful force and can make a significant difference in this world through your actions. Believe it, embrace it, and let it propel you forward on your journey of purpose and impact.

Day 14

But those who hope in the Lord will renew their strength.
They will soar on wings like eagles; they will run and
not grow weary, they will walk and not be faint.

—Isaiah 40:31

I am a young boy, teenager, of melanin who refuses to be defined by the fears and doubts of this world. In a society that often fails to recognize our worth, I find solace and strength in the words of Isaiah 40:31. I am reminded that those who trust in the Lord will renew their strength. The expectations or judgments of others do not limit me. I am valuable, capable, and deserving of love and respect.

I rise above the noise and negativity surrounding me, for the promises of God empower me. I am filled with a renewed sense of purpose and determination. I walk confidently, knowing that God has a unique plan and purpose for my life.

I refuse to allow the opinions of others to define me. I embrace my individuality, knowing that my differences make me extraordinary. I use my voice to uplift and inspire others, showing them that they, too, are worthy of love, respect, and success.

In a world that often seeks to tear us down, I stand tall, knowing that the superficial standards of this world do not determine my worth. I am fearfully and wonderfully made and embrace the truth that I am enough. I am a beacon of light, shining brightly in a world desperately needing hope and encouragement.

I walk in the confidence and strength of the Lord, for His love and acceptance are unwavering. I am a young boy, teenager, or man who believes in his worth, purpose, and ability to make a difference. I am unshakable, for I trust in the promises of Isaiah 40:31.

Day 15

Do not be anxious about anything, but in everything
by prayer and supplication with thanksgiving, let
your requests be made known to God.

—Philippians 4:6

I am a young boy, teenager, or young man of melanin who refuses to succumb to the negativity and setbacks plaguing our society. Even in the face of killings, negative stereotypes, and social and economic setbacks, I find strength and hope in the words of Philippians 4:6.

I choose to rise above the challenges surrounding me, knowing I am not alone in my struggles. I bring my fears, worries, and frustrations before God, trusting He will provide me with the peace and guidance I need.

The violence or negativity in this world does not define me. I strive to be a force of positive change, spreading love, understanding, and unity wherever I go. I reject the stereotypes others may place upon me, knowing that my character and actions truly define me.

In the face of social and economic setbacks, I refuse to be discouraged. I believe in my potential and capability to overcome any obstacle that stands in my way. I am determined to work hard, pursue my dreams, and strive for success, for I know that my efforts will not be in vain.

I am resilient, strong, and capable of achieving greatness. I refuse to let the negativity around me hinder my progress. Instead, I use it as fuel to propel me to prove to myself and others that I can rise above the challenges I face.

I am a young boy, teenager, or young man who believes in his ability to create positive change in this world. I trust in God's plan for my life, knowing He is with me every step. I embrace the power of Philippians 4:6, allowing it to guide me toward a future filled with success, purpose, and fulfillment.

Day 16

"For I know the plans I have for you," declares
the Lord, "plans to prosper you and not to harm
you, plans to give you hope and a future."

—Jeremiah 29:11

I am a young boy, teenager, or young man of melanin living in a world that often misunderstands and fears me. Despite this, I find solace and strength in the words of Jeremiah 29:11.

I believe that God has a plan for my life, one that is filled with hope, purpose, and a future beyond what I can imagine. I refuse to let the judgments and misconceptions of others define my worth.

In moments when I feel unseen or undervalued, I remind myself that God sees and knows me intimately. He understands my struggles, my pain, and my emotions. I am not alone in my journey, for He walks beside me, providing comfort, guidance, and unconditional love.

I am not defined by the circumstances or challenges that I face within my family or in life. Instead, I choose to grow from these experiences, using them as stepping stones toward becoming the best version of myself.

I acknowledge that dealing with emotions can be overwhelming at times, but I embrace the fact that it is okay to feel and express them. I seek healthy outlets to process and manage my emotions, whether it be through prayer, talking to trusted individuals, or engaging in activities that bring me joy and peace.

I am resilient, capable, and worthy of love and respect. I refuse to let the negative perceptions of society diminish my self-worth. Instead, I strive to be a positive influence, embracing my unique qualities and using them to uplift and inspire others.

I trust in the plan that God has for me, even when it feels uncertain or challenging. I know that He will provide me with the strength and guidance I need to navigate through life's obstacles. I am a young boy, teenager, or young man with a purpose, and I am determined to live a life that reflects my worth and potential.

Day 17

The Lord is my light and my salvation—whom shall I fear? The Lord is the stronghold of my life—of whom shall I be afraid?"

—Psalm 27:1

As a young boy, teenager, or young adult of melanin, I affirm to you my beautiful child of melanin:

1. Your melanin is beautiful and unique, a reflection of the diversity and richness of your heritage.
2. You are fearfully and wonderfully made, deserving of respect, love, and acceptance.
3. Refuse to internalize the negative stereotypes and biases projected onto you. Define your own worth and potential.
4. You're not limited by the expectations of others. You are capable of achieving greatness, breaking barriers, and shattering glass ceilings.
5. Embrace your emotions and use them as fuel for growth and resilience. You are allowed to feel and express yourself authentically.
6. You are not defined by society's narrow standards of beauty. Celebrate your natural features and embrace your own unique style.
7. You are intelligent, talented, and capable of excelling in any field you choose. You are a beacon of knowledge and wisdom.
8. You are a leader, inspiring others with your actions, words, and positive influence. You have the power to make a difference in our community and beyond.

9. You are worthy of love, healthy relationships, and a fulfilling life. My child, surround yourself with people who uplift and support you.

10. You are resilient and capable of overcoming any obstacle that comes your way. I encourage you to embrace challenges as opportunities for growth and learning.

11. My child of melanin, take pride in your cultural heritage and contribute to its preservation and celebration. My prince, honor the sacrifices of those who came before you.

12. You are a voice for change, advocating for equality, justice, and representation. My child of great strength, use your platform to amplify marginalized voices.

13. You are not limited by societal expectations or stereotypes. You are free to pursue your passions, dreams, and aspirations without apology.

14. You are deserving of success, happiness, and fulfillment. Work hard, my beautiful prince, work to persevere and seize every opportunity that comes your way.

15. You are a force to be reckoned with, breaking down barriers and challenging systemic injustices. You are a catalyst for positive change.

Day 18

The righteous cry out, and the Lord hears them;
he delivers them from all their troubles.

—Psalm 34:17

As a young boy/teenager/young man, I affirm that the Lord hears your cries in times of difficulty and challenge. He listens to your prayers and knows the depths of your heart. Even in moments of feeling alone or misunderstood, God sees and understands you completely. He is always by your side, aware of your struggles. When your heart is broken or burdened, the Lord is close to you, offering comfort, healing, and strength during times of sadness or pain. In moments of family troubles or conflicts, God becomes your refuge and safe haven, providing wisdom and guidance to navigate through difficult situations. As you encounter trials and obstacles in life, trust that the Lord will deliver you from them all. He equips you with resilience, courage, and determination to overcome any challenge that comes your way. You am not defined by your mistakes or short-comings but rather by the grace and forgiveness of God, who loves you unconditionally. The Lord surrounds you with His angels, protecting you from harm and guiding you toward a path of righteousness and purpose. With His strength and power, you are empowered to resist negative influences and temptations, make wise choices, and stand firm in your values. You must have faith that He is working all things together for your good. Embrace the truth you are a vessel of God's love and a light in this world. Through your actions, words, and deeds, you have the power to make a positive impact and bring hope to those around you. May these affirmations based on Psalms

34:17 inspire and uplift you, young boys, teenagers, and young men, reminding you of your worth, strength, and the unwavering love of God that surrounds you.

Day 19

Come to me, all you who are weary and burdened, and I will give you rest. Take my yoke upon you and learn from me, for I am gentle and humble in heart, and you will find rest for your souls. For my yoke is easy and my burden is light

—Matthew 11:28–30

Attention, young boys, teenagers, and young men: take comfort in the words of Matthew 11:28–30.

You may be facing various challenges and pressures in your life, whether it's school, relationships, or figuring out your identity and purpose. But know that Jesus extends an open invitation to you. He wants you to come to Him with all your weariness and burdens. He promises to give you rest.

In a world that often demands so much from you, Jesus offers a different way. He invites you to take His yoke upon yourself and learn from Him. His ways are gentle and humble, and by following Him, you will find rest for your souls.

Remember, you don't have to carry the weight of the world on your shoulders alone. Jesus understands your struggles and is ready to help you navigate through them. Trust in His words and lean on Him for support. His yoke is easy to bear, and His burden is light.

Take a moment to reflect on these verses and find solace in the presence of Jesus. Allow His love and grace to guide you through this season of your life. You are not alone, and with Him, you will find the strength and rest you need.

Day 20

No, in all these things we are more than
conquerors through him who loved us.

—Romans 8:37

Dear young boys, teenagers, and young men of melanin, let the words of Romans 8:37 be a source of encouragement and affirmation for you: "No, in all these things we are more than conquerors through him who loved us."

Living in a world that may not always recognize your worth or acknowledge the challenges you face can be disheartening. You may sometimes feel misunderstood, overlooked, or even scared. But remember, you are more than conquerors through the love of Jesus Christ.

Don't allow the negativity or fear surrounding you to define your identity. Instead, embrace the truth that you are loved by a God who sees your value and potential. He is with you every step of the way, empowering you to overcome any obstacles that come your way.

Family, life, and personal struggles can sometimes feel overwhelming, leaving you with a whirlwind of emotions. It's essential to acknowledge and process these emotions, understanding that it is okay to seek support and guidance when needed. Don't let pride or societal expectations prevent you from seeking help.

Remember, you are not alone in your journey. Reach out to trusted family members, mentors, or friends who can offer guidance and a listening ear. Additionally, find solace in prayer and seek God's wisdom and strength to navigate through life's challenges.

Embrace your unique experiences and insights about life. Your perspective is valuable and can contribute to positive change in the world around you. Your voice matters, and your actions can make a difference.

Stay rooted in your faith, knowing that you have been equipped to overcome it. Embrace your worth, walk with confidence, and strive to be a light in a world that may sometimes seem dark. Through God's love, you can rise above any adversity and fulfill your purpose.

You are more than conquerors, dear young prince. Embrace this truth, hold your head high, and strive to make a positive impact in your life and the lives of others.

Day 21

I lift up my eyes to the mountains—where does
my help come from? My help comes from the
Lord, the Maker of heaven and earth.

—Psalm 121:1–2

Dear boys of melanin, take comfort in the words of Psalm 121:1–2 as an affirmation that celebrates your unique identity and encourages you to stand tall without assimilation:

I lift up my eyes to the mountains—
Where does my help come from?
My help comes from the Lord,
the Maker of heaven and earth.

In a world that may pressure you to assimilate or conform to certain standards, remember that your worth and strength come from the Lord who created you. Lift your eyes to the mountains, symbolizing the greatness and majesty of God, and recognize that your help and identity are found in Him alone.

You are fearfully and wonderfully made, each with your own distinct heritage, culture, and experiences. Embrace your heritage with pride, knowing that it contributes to the beautiful tapestry of humanity. Do not let society's expectations or prejudices dictate how you see yourself or how you should navigate through life.

Your melanin is a testament to the diversity and richness of God's creation. It is a part of your identity that should be celebrated and cherished. Embrace the beauty of your skin, hair, and features, for they are uniquely yours.

As you walk through life, remember that you do not need to assimilate or conform to fit into a mold that society may pressure you to embrace. Instead, walk confidently in your own identity, being true to who you are and the values that you hold dear.

Seek strength and guidance from the Lord, who understands and affirms your unique experiences. Lean on Him for support, wisdom, and assurance as you navigate the challenges and obstacles that may come your way.

Surround yourself with a community that uplifts and supports you, a community that celebrates diversity and stands against discrimination. Together, you can create a world that embraces and values the beauty of each individual, regardless of their skin color or background.

Hold your head high, dear boys of melanin, and know that you are fearfully and wonderfully made. Your worth, strength, and identity come from the Lord. Embrace your heritage, stand firm in your convictions, and be a beacon of light in a world that needs your unique voice and perspective.

You are loved, valued, and accepted just as you are. Walk confidently, knowing that your worth and identity are rooted in your Creator.

With love and encouragement, may you always remember that your melanin is not a burden to bear but a source of strength and resilience. It is a reminder of the rich history and heritage that flows through your veins. Embrace it, celebrate it, and let it be a beacon of pride that shines brightly wherever you go.

In a world that may try to dim your light, remember that you are not called to assimilate but to shine boldly as your authentic self. Your unique experiences, perspectives, and talents have the power to shape and change the world around you.

Do not be discouraged by those who may try to define you by narrow standards or limit your potential. You are capable of greatness beyond measure, and your worth extends far beyond external appearances.

As you navigate through life, know that you are not alone. The Lord, the Maker of heaven and earth, walks beside you every step of the way. He sees your struggles, hears your prayers, and delights in your successes.

Seek solace in His presence and find strength in His promises. Allow His love to fill your heart, reminding you that you are beautifully and wonderfully made in His image. You are a masterpiece, intricately designed with purpose and intention.

Embrace your unique journey, for it is in the intersections of your identity that your true power lies. Your voice, your story, and your contributions matter. They have the potential to break down barriers, challenge stereotypes, and inspire others to embrace their own identities unapologetically.

Prime boys of melanin, remember that your melanin is not a limitation but a gift. It is a reminder of the strength, resilience, and beauty that flows through your veins. Embrace your heritage, stand tall in your identity, and let your light shine brightly for all to see.

You are powerful, you are loved, and you are an essential part of the tapestry of humanity. Never forget the truth of Psalm 121:1–2, and let it be a constant affirmation that strengthens and uplifts you throughout your journey.

With unwavering support and admiration, May you always recognize that your melanin is a symbol of the vibrant cultures and histories that have shaped the world. It is a badge of honor, a testament to the resilience and triumphs of your ancestors. Embrace it as a reminder of the beauty and diversity that exists within our global community.

In a society that may try to diminish your worth, remember that you are deserving of respect, dignity, and equal opportunities. Do not allow anyone to undermine your dreams or limit your potential. Your talents, intelligence, and creativity are boundless, and they have the power to create positive change in the world.

As you navigate through life, surround yourself with a community that uplifts and supports you. Seek out mentors who have walked a similar path and can offer guidance and wisdom. Together, you can create a network of strength and solidarity that will propel you toward success.

Remember that your worth is not determined by external validation or societal norms. Your value lies in your character, your compassion, and your ability to make a difference in the lives of others.

Your melanin is just one facet of your identity, and it does not define your entire being. Embrace all aspects of yourself and take pride in the unique qualities that make you who you are.

In times of struggle or self-doubt, draw strength from your heritage and the stories of those who came before you. They overcame countless obstacles and paved the way for you to thrive. Let their resilience and determination inspire you to persevere and never give up on your dreams.

Above all, remember that you are worthy of love and happiness. Your melanin is a part of your beauty, and it should be celebrated, cherished, and protected. Embrace your melanin as a source of strength, dignity, and power, and let it be a reminder of the greatness that lies within you.

Day 22

Even though I walk through the darkest valley, I will fear no evil,
for you are with me; your rod and your staff, they comfort me.

—Psalm 23:4

Even in a world where my worth may be judged by my skin, find solace in the words of Psalm 23:4, deep within.

Though you may walk through valleys of prejudice and strife, be confident, for God is with you, guiding your life. No matter the judgments or biases that surround you, you affirm your worth, knowing your Creator's love is profound. Your value is not defined by the color of your skin but by the content of your character and the love you bring within.

In the face of adversity, stand tall and strong, for you are resilient and courageous, and you belong. You are worthy of love, respect, and equal rights. No matter the darkness that tries to dim your lights. Embrace your heritage, your culture, and your soul, for they make you unique, complete, and whole.

You are to rise above the limitations society may impose, For your worth is not determined by external foes. With confidence in your heart and faith in your stride, you are to navigate this world, letting your inner light guide me. You are more than the judgments that others may cast, for you are fearfully and wonderfully made, unsurpassed. In the presence of God, you find strength and grace. Knowing that your worth is not defined by the world's embrace.

I affirm my confidence, despite the challenges you may face, for in God's love, your worth is firmly in place. So stand tall, empowered, and beautifully embracing your worth and letting your spirit soar free, for you are worthy, cherished, and deserving of all in a world where your skin may try to make you small. May this affirmation strengthen your resolve and remind you that your worth is never to be dissolved, for you are confident, even in a world that may to discredit you try. To determine your worth based on your skin, you defy.

Day 23

For the Spirit God gave us does not make us timid,
but gives us power, love and self-discipline
In the face of challenges, I stand strong and bold.

—Second Timothy 1:7

For I am a young man of melanin, fearlessly I'm told. With the words of 2 Timothy 1:7 deep within my heart, I affirm my confidence, knowing God's power won't depart. I refuse to be timid. I embrace my strength and might, for God's spirit within me shines eternally bright. In a world that may doubt me, I choose to trust in Him, knowing that His love and power will never dim. I am not defined by the color of my skin but by the content of my character deep within.

I rise above stereotypes and societal expectations, for God's purpose and destiny are my true foundations. With courage in my heart and faith in my stride, I navigate life's journey, letting God be my guide. I am worthy of respect, love, and success, For God's favor upon me is boundless, no less.

I excel in my endeavors, embracing my unique gifts, Knowing that through Christ, my spirit forever lifts. I walk with confidence, leaving timidity behind, For in God's strength, true greatness I find.

I am a young man of melanin, with a divine purpose, shattering barriers, and letting my light shine brightly. I embrace my heritage, my culture, and my voice. Knowing that in God's plan, I have an important choice.

I stand tall and proud, defying any limitation, for I am fearfully and wonderfully made, a true creation. So I trust in God's power, His love, and grace. Knowing that through Him, I'll triumph in every race.

With 2 Timothy 1:7 as my affirmation and guide, I am a young man of melanin, unstoppable, and dignified. I am confident, bold, and unshakable in my faith, for God's strength within me, no obstacle can wraith. I trust in Him completely, for He's always by my side, empowering me to walk in purpose, with Him as my guide.

When you pass through the waters, I will be with you;
and when you pass through the rivers, they will not sweep
over you. When you walk through the fire, you will
not be burned; the flames will not set you ablaze.

—Isaiah 43:2

Through the storms and trials, I declare with might, as a young man of melanin, I won't give up the fight. Isaiah 43:2 reminds me of God's unwavering grace. His steadfast love, I find the strength to embrace.

When waters rise and troubles surround me, I hold firm to the promise. I won't be drowned, for God is with me, even in the midst of strife. He's my refuge and fortress, the source of my life.

Though the flames may rage and scorch my path, I trust in God's protection, shielding me from wrath. With resilience in my heart and faith in my soul,

I press on with determination, achieving my goals. I refuse to be discouraged or wallow in despair, for God's presence is constant. He'll always be there.

In times of adversity, I am not alone, for God walks beside me, making His presence known. He will guide me through the darkest night, leading me toward the dawn with His radiant light.

I am a young man of melanin, strong and bold.

With Isaiah 43:2, I anchor my soul, never to fold. No matter the obstacles or challenges I face, God's strength within me will help me embrace it. I will persevere. I will rise above. With God's love and power, I'll conquer and prove.

I am resilient, courageous, and steadfast in my belief, For through tough times, God's grace brings relief. I trust in His plan,

His purpose, His way, knowing that He'll never leave or lead me astray.

So I declare with unwavering faith and fervor,

As a young man of melanin, I'll never surrender. With Isaiah 43:2 as my guiding light, I face every trial, standing tall, ready to fight. Through the storms and fires, I will endure, for in God's hands, my victory is secure.

Day 25

The Lord is my light and my salvation: whom shall I fear? The Lord is the stronghold of my life: of whom shall I be afraid?

—Psalm 27:1

I am fearfully and wonderfully made, a young man of melanin, blessed with the richness of my heritage and the brilliance of my potential. In a world that sometimes tries to dim my light, I stand tall, embracing the power of my melanin and the strength it represents.

I affirm that my melanin is not a burden but a badge of honor, a symbol of resilience, and a testament to the beauty that lies within me. It is a reminder of the countless generations that have come before me, who have triumphed over adversity and paved the way for my success.

I declare that my melanin is not a limitation but a catalyst for greatness. It fuels my determination, ignites my passion, and propels me forward. It is a source of inspiration that drives me to exceed expectations, break down barriers, and shatter stereotypes.

I affirm that my melanin is not a source of shame but a source of pride. I celebrate the richness of my culture, the diversity of my community, and the unity that comes from embracing our differences. I am a vessel of change, a voice for justice, and a beacon of hope for those who may feel marginalized.

I declare that my melanin is not a definition of who I am but a part of the mosaic that makes me unique. It intertwines with my character, my values, my dreams, and my aspirations. It empowers me to stand firm in my convictions, strive for excellence, and to make a positive impact in the world.

I affirm that my melanin is not a burden to bear alone but a shared journey with my brothers, my friends, and my community.

Together, we uplift one another, support one another, and amplify our voices. We stand in solidarity, embracing our melanin with pride and working toward a world where equality and justice prevail.

I declare that my melanin is a gift, a blessing that I will cherish, nurture, and use to uplift others. With the Lord as my refuge and salvation, I know that I am fearfully and wonderfully made. I am a young man of melanin, destined for greatness, and I will rise above every obstacle that comes my way.

Day 26

Be on your guard; stand firm in the faith; be courageous; be strong.

—First Corinthians 16:13

I am a young boy of melanin, fearfully and wonderfully made by a loving and powerful God. Despite what others may say, believe, or do to me, I choose to stand firm in my faith and remain steadfast and unmovable.

I affirm that God's love and purpose for me are unwavering, regardless of the challenges I may face. I am a team player with God, allowing His strength and guidance to empower me in every situation.

I declare that I am not defined by the negative words or actions of others. Instead, I am defined by my character, my integrity, and my unwavering faith in God. I choose to rise above the negativity, embracing God's promises and walking in His truth.

I affirm that I am courageous and strong, relying on God's strength to navigate through life's obstacles. I will not be discouraged or shaken by what others may say or do to me. With God by my side, I am capable of achieving greatness and making a positive impact in the world.

I declare that I am a team player with God, trusting in His divine plan for my life. I will seek His guidance, wisdom, and direction in all that I do. I am open to His leading, knowing that He will equip me with everything I need to fulfill my purpose.

I affirm that I am steadfast and unmovable in my faith, rooted in God's love and grace. I will not be swayed by the opinions or prejudices of others. Instead, I will stand strong, knowing that God's love for me is unwavering and His plans for me are good.

I declare that I will persevere and overcome any challenges that come my way, knowing that God is with me every step of the journey. I am a young boy of melanin, chosen and loved by God, and I will walk confidently in His promises, shining His light in a world that needs it.

Day 27

Cast all your anxiety on him because he cares for you.

—First Peter 5:7

As a young boy of melanin, I acknowledge that there are many things beyond my control that may cause panic and worry. However, I choose to cast all my anxiety upon God, for He cares deeply for me.

I affirm that God's love for me is unwavering, and His care is limitless. In times of uncertainty and fear, I will surrender my worries to Him, knowing that He is attentive to my every concern.

I declare that I will not be overwhelmed by the things I cannot control. Instead, I will place my trust in God, knowing that He holds my future in His hands. I believe that He has a purpose and a plan for my life, and He will guide me through every challenge and obstacle.

I affirm that God's presence brings peace to my heart and mind. I will seek His comfort and guidance through prayer and meditation on His Word. I trust that as I cast my anxieties upon Him, He will provide me with the strength and courage I need to face each day.

I declare that I am not alone in my struggles. God is with me, walking beside me every step of the way. His love and care for me are constant, and I can rely on Him to carry me through any difficulty.

I affirm that I am fearfully and wonderfully made, created in the image of God. I will not allow external circumstances or societal pressures to define my worth. Instead, I will embrace my identity as a young boy of melanin, knowing that I am valued and cherished by my Heavenly Father.

I declare that I will trust God wholeheartedly, knowing that He is faithful to fulfill His promises. I will not be consumed by panic or worry, but I will rest in the assurance that God is in control. He will provide for my needs and guide me toward a future filled with hope and purpose.

I affirm that as I surrender my anxieties to God, I will experience His peace that surpasses all understanding. His peace will guard my heart and mind, allowing me to navigate life's challenges with confidence and grace.

I declare that I am a child of God, and I will trust in His unfailing love and care. I will cast all my anxieties upon Him, knowing that He will sustain me and carry me through every season of life.

Day 28

The God who made the world and everything in it—he is Lord
of heaven and earth—does not live in shrines made by hands.
Neither is he served by human hands, as though he needed
anything, since he himself gives everyone life and breath and
all things. From one man he has made every nationality to
live over the whole earth and has determined their appointed
times and the boundaries of where they live. He did this so
that they might seek God, and perhaps they might reach out
and find him, though he is not far from each one of us.

—Acts 17:24–27, CSB

I affirm that the God who made the world and everything in it is
the Lord of heaven and earth. He does not dwell in shrines made by
human hands, for He is beyond the limits of our physical constructs.
He is not served by human hands, for He is self-sufficient and lacks
nothing. It is He who gives us life, breath, and all things.

I declare that God, in His infinite wisdom, has created every
nationality to inhabit the entire earth. He has determined their
appointed times and the boundaries of where they live. This divine
orchestration serves a purpose: to lead us to seek after Him, to reach
out and find Him.

I affirm that God is not far from each one of us, regardless of our
nationality or the color of our skin. He is intimately present in our lives,
always within our reach. He desires for us, boys of melanin, to seek Him
and discover the depth of His love, grace, and purpose for our lives.

I declare that as boys of melanin, we are fearfully and wonderfully
made by our Creator. Our worth and value are not defined by societal
standards or the opinions of others. We are cherished and loved by
God, who has intentionally placed us in this world at this specific time.

I affirm that God's presence in our lives brings hope, strength, and resilience. In moments of adversity and challenges, we can turn to Him for guidance and comfort. He will equip us to overcome obstacles and walk in the fullness of our potential.

I declare that as boys of melanin, we have a unique role to play in the grand tapestry of humanity. Our diverse backgrounds and experiences contribute to the richness of this world. We are called to embrace our identity, celebrate our heritage, and use our voices to advocate for justice, equality, and unity.

I affirm that God's purpose for our lives extends beyond the limitations imposed by others. We are not confined by stereotypes or societal expectations. In God's eyes, we are limitless, capable of achieving greatness and making a positive impact in our communities and beyond.

I declare that as boys of melanin, we are part of a global family. We stand united with our brothers and sisters from every nation, knowing that we are all created in the image of God. Together, we can seek Him, grow in His love and grace, and create a brighter future for generations to come.

I affirm that God's love knows no boundaries or divisions. He embraces and celebrates the beauty of our melanin, for it is part of His intricate design. We are fearfully and wonderfully made, and we will walk confidently in our purpose, shining our light in a world that needs our unique contributions.

Day 29

God has determined the "appointed times
and the boundaries" of our existence.

—Acts 17:26, CSB

I affirm that the times and boundaries of our existence as boys of melanin are divinely placed and purposed by the hands of God Himself. In both moments of joy and moments of hardship, we can find peace knowing that God has orchestrated our journey.

I declare that our existence is not a coincidence or a mistake. We are fearfully and wonderfully made with a purpose that goes beyond societal expectations or limitations. Our melanin is a beautiful part of God's design, reflecting His creativity and diversity.

I affirm that God's divine timing is at work in our lives. Every step we take, every challenge we face, and every success we achieve is part of His greater plan. We can trust that He has equipped us with the strength and resilience to navigate through all circumstances.

I declare that our melanin is not a burden but a gift. It carries the legacy of our ancestors, their strength, and their triumphs. It is a reminder of the rich heritage that we inherit and the potential we have to make a difference in our communities and the world.

I affirm that during the good times, we will celebrate the blessings and victories in our lives, acknowledging that they come from the hand of God. We will use our successes as a platform to inspire and uplift others, knowing that our purpose extends beyond our personal achievements.

I declare that during the hard times, we will find solace in the knowledge that God is with us. His presence brings comfort and peace, reminding us that we are not alone in our struggles. We will persevere, knowing that our melanin does not define our worth, but rather, it is our character and resilience that shine through.

I affirm that as boys of melanin, we have the power to break stereotypes and defy expectations. We will rise above the limitations that others may try to impose on us, knowing that our true worth is found in our relationship with God and the potential He has placed within us.

I declare that we will embrace our identity as boys of melanin, celebrating the beauty of our skin and the diversity it represents. We will stand tall, united with our brothers and sisters, knowing that our collective strength and unity can bring about positive change in our communities and the world.

I affirm that as boys of melanin, we are part of a larger story. Our lives matter, our voices matter, and our contributions matter. We will strive for excellence, pursuing education, leadership, and personal growth, knowing that we have the power to impact future generations.

I declare that we will walk boldly in our purpose, knowing that the times and boundaries of our existence are divinely ordained. With God as our guide, we will navigate through life with confidence, grace, and the unwavering belief that we are fearfully and wonderfully made.

Day 30

Be very careful how you live. Do not live like those who are not wise. Live wisely. I mean that you should use every chance you have for doing good, because these are evil times. So do not be foolish with your lives. But learn what the Lord wants you to do.

—Ephesians 5:15–17, ICB

I affirm that as boys of melanin, we understand the importance of living wisely and using our time for good. We recognize that these are challenging times, but we refuse to be foolish with our lives. Instead, we commit to learning what the Lord wants us to do and making a positive impact in the world.

I declare that we will be intentional in managing our time, recognizing that it is a precious resource that directly impacts our lives and the legacy we leave behind. We will prioritize our time, focusing on activities that align with our values, goals, and the greater purpose that God has placed within us.

I affirm that we will not be swayed by distractions or the pressures of society. We will guard our time and use it wisely, refusing to waste it on meaningless pursuits or negative influences. Instead, we will invest our time in personal growth, education, and pursuing our passions.

I declare that we will seek wisdom and guidance from the Lord in how to best utilize our time. We will spend time in prayer, seeking His direction and understanding His will for our lives. We will listen to His voice and follow His leading, knowing that He has a specific plan and purpose for each of us.

I affirm that we will seize every opportunity to do good and make a difference in the lives of others. We will use our time to serve, uplift, and empower those around us, especially within our communities. We will be agents of positive change, using our voices and actions to bring about justice and equality.

I declare that as boys of melanin, we will not be limited by societal expectations or stereotypes. We will use our time to challenge and break down barriers, advocating for inclusivity, diversity, and equal opportunities for all. We will be trailblazers, inspiring future generations to rise above limitations and strive for greatness.

I affirm that our time is valuable and holds the potential to create a lasting impact. We will make the most of every moment, cherishing the present and embracing the opportunities that come our way. We will live each day with purpose, knowing that the legacy we leave behind is shaped by how we use our time.

I declare that as boys of melanin, we understand that our time is a gift from God. We will steward it well, honoring Him with our actions and choices. We will seek to glorify Him in all that we do, knowing that our time on earth is a chance to make His love and grace known to others.

I affirm that as boys of melanin, we are capable of achieving great things when we manage our time wisely. We will not be limited by societal expectations or circumstances. Instead, we will rise above and create a legacy that inspires and uplifts generations to come.

Day 31

Whoever walks in integrity walks securely, but
whoever takes crooked paths will be found out.

—Proverbs 10:9, NIV

I affirm that as boys of melanin, we understand the importance of walking with integrity. We recognize that our actions, both in public and in private, should align with the values that are in our hearts. We choose to live a life of honesty, transparency, and moral uprightness.

I declare that we will not take crooked paths or engage in dishonest practices. We understand that true integrity means being true to ourselves, to others, and to God. We will uphold our values and make decisions that align with what is right, even when it may be difficult or unpopular.

I affirm that we will be accountable for our actions and choices. We understand that integrity is not about fooling others but about being true to ourselves and to God. We will examine our motives and intentions, ensuring that they are pure and honorable.

I declare that we will strive to build and maintain strong relationships based on trust and respect. We understand that integrity is the foundation of healthy connections with others. We will treat others with fairness, kindness, and honesty, valuing their trust and working to earn it.

I affirm that we will not compromise our biblical values for temporary gain or pleasure. We understand that when we violate our principles, there are consequences that can harm not only ourselves but also those around us. We will choose to live a life that aligns with God's word, seeking His guidance and wisdom in all that we do.

I declare that as boys of melanin, we will be examples of integrity within our communities. We will inspire others to walk securely and to make choices that honor God and reflect their true character. We will stand up against injustice and corruption, promoting honesty, transparency, and ethical behavior.

I affirm that our integrity will be a source of strength and confidence. We understand that walking with integrity allows us to live with peace of mind and a clear conscience. We will not be swayed by the temptations of dishonesty or deceit, but instead, we will stand firm in our commitment to live with integrity.

I declare that as boys of melanin, we are capable of living lives of integrity that leave a positive and lasting impact. We will strive to be men of character, known for our honesty, reliability, and moral uprightness. Our integrity will shine forth as a beacon of light, inspiring others to follow in our footsteps.

I affirm that our commitment to integrity will not waver. We will continue to grow and mature in our understanding and practice of integrity, recognizing that it is a lifelong journey. We will seek God's guidance and rely on His strength to help us walk securely in integrity every day of our lives.

About the Author

Revered Dr. Yvette A. Armstead is a native of Mobile, Alabama. She relocated to New York twenty-one years ago. The challenge from moving to New York was a big transition. She received her bachelor's degree from the University of South Alabama her MBA in Public Health Administration from Colorado Technical University. She has her PhD in Christian Counseling from Louisiana Baptist  University and Seminary and she is currently pursuing a Doctor of Ministry degree in Missional Leadership for Pittsburgh Theological Seminary. She is the proud mother of three children, LeBrandon, Azaria, and Antonio, and one granddaughter, Lyric. In her spare time, she enjoys spending time alone, reading, walking and traveling.